T0124719

# THE KNIVES OF VILLALEJO

# Matthew
# Stewart

# The
# Knives
# of
EYEWEAR PUBLISHING
# Villalejo

First published in 2017
by Eyewear Publishing Ltd
Suite 333, 19-21 Crawford Street
Marylebone, London w1h 1pj
United Kingdom

*Cover design and typeset by* Edwin Smet
*Author photograph by* Marina Rodríguez

*Printed in England by* TJ International Ltd, Padstow, Cornwall

*All rights reserved*
© 2017 Matthew Stewart

The right of Matthew Stewart to be identified as author of
this work has been asserted in accordance with section 77
of the Copyright, Designs and Patents Act 1988

isbn 978-1-911335-63-4

*Eyewear wishes to thank Jonathan Wonham for his
generous patronage of our press.*

WWW.EYEWEARPUBLISHING.COM

For Marina

Matthew Stewart
lives between West Sussex and
Extremadura. Following a comprehensive
school education, he took a degree in Modern
Languages at St Peter's College, Oxford.
He works in the Spanish wine trade and has
published two pamphlets with HappenStance
Press (*Inventing Truth*, 2011 and *Tasting Notes*,
2012). He runs poetry blog Rogue Strands
and has been published in *Ambit*,
*London Magazine* and *The Rialto*.
This is his first full collection.

# TABLE OF CONTENTS

*No aceptar otro orden que el de las afinidades, otra cronología que la del corazón, otro horario que el de los encuentros a deshora, los verdaderos.*

No accepting of any order other than affinities, any chronology other than the heart, any schedule other than encounters at an inappropriate time, the true ones.

— Julio Cortázar

# FORMICA

(i)

An ochre dusk through the window,
stewed apples sighing from the hob
and slippers squeaking back and forth
on the lino – Mum's become Gran,
Son now Dad, but a boy still plays
at the same Formica table.
This kitchen's hub, its ersatz knots
are giving off a perfect shine.

(ii)

The empty chair is staring hungrily
while I eat my pasta, each spoonful tracked
by the arching slats and tethered cushion,
by the almost eyes of the almost you,
by trees swaying through your almost torso
and clouds converging with your almost hair.

## YOU'VE REACHED 020...

I dial and dial, never leave a message,
what I dread is your picking up one day
and your voice turning unpredictable.

I love to hear it tinny, caught on tape,
giving a number rather than a name,
as if you were the prisoner, not me.

# MILKO

Bottles chimed on the doorstep.
By the ebbs and surges of daily pints
you knew who'd grown, who'd aged, who'd upped and left.
Your float's low hum was the routine soundtrack
to Ready Brek, wonky ties and dull dawns.

Undercut by out-of-towns,
you'll be my generation's pie 'n' mash,
a tale suffered by countless grandchildren
while something else is also dying out
and patiently rehearsing for your role.

# IN THE FRIDGE

When we make an unexpected visit,
bricked-up walls of butter or half-drunk wine
or three tomatoes spliced and forgotten
say all we need to know about her month.

When we get back, I haul our cases up,
you rush to the shop for bacon and milk.
A full fridge, and the flat will be our home:
I water plants, you load the shelves, we touch.

# STRAIGHT FROM THE AIRPORT

My fingertips shudder
by your bed. I tell you
how David did in Maths,
how his forehand's flowing
perfectly. Anything
to forget the smoothness
of your twitching cheek.

I read the night away
in time to your wrenched breaths
as if the plot could turn,
could end on a flashback.
You're home, scooping me up
from my book to the rasp
of your fresh stubble.

# SOONER OR LATER

For the moment it skulks
below forgotten gifts
and out-of-favour shirts
in the spare-room wardrobe.

Maybe tonight, maybe
next year, a sudden call
will bring it centre stage,
rushed to the dry cleaners.

They'll hanger it. Shoulders
will thrust like instructions
for use. There's not a hope
of dodging the dark suit.

# INSTRUCTIONS FOR COMING HOME

Your fingers will have to trespass
through umpteen kitchen drawers. Let them.
The gas rings will purr. That's their sound.
Hack at a spud. Defy its eyes
with your knife. Crack eggs and watch them
splutter. You'll remember this smell
used to greet you at the front door.
Lever them free, the spatula
no less a tool than any spade.
Now confront the day, bite by bite.

# 01252 722698

(i)
You worked your way round my milk teeth,
sung countless times before you stuck.
Soon a chameleonic code,
you were my safeguard from a snatch,
then my duty when staying out
and recently a thankful leap
from trade fairs and dogged insects.
My fingers refuse to leave you.


(ii)
I disembark
at an airport
or lock the door
in my latest hotel
or hug the bed
on getting home

and fingers reach
for that number
until they shrink
into a sudden fist
as if hoping
I won't notice.

# RE-EMERGENCE

Among the criss-crossing shoppers,
I spot you: the curve of your jaw,
slope of your shoulders in a queue
or slow stoop to a shelf at Boots.

My steps stall, the back of my neck
sparks, a smile about to break out.
The angle opens. A stranger
glances through me.

# DEBRIS

(i)
*At the dump*

*Small electrical, mate?* A grin,
and he reaches for the shaver,
hurls it high into the skip.

Back at the car, you're lingering.
My knuckles crampon round the wheel,
coated in dusty stubble.

(ii)
*3B*

Thoughts are unloading when the pen conks out,
but a dark rummage locates your pencil
perfectly wigwammed by a Stanley knife,

and words have scampered across the paper,
racing against the tip before it blunts
and a sharpener peels your work away.

(iii)
*The touch*

My address book reproaches me daily.
I used to leaf it, stroking squares of ink
where exes had been. The dead were crossed out
and their kids or spouses placed alongside.
Not anymore. Your malingering name
vanished today at the touch of a screen.

# THE 23<sup>RD</sup>

*in memory of George Stewart*


It casually loiters in the fourth line
of April, pretending not to stalk me,
the expiry date on David's passport
and the start of a trade fair in Brussels.
It knows full well you chose your namesake's day
to die, as if you were somehow afraid
I might forget. As if I ever could.

## LA DESPEDIDA

There's a regular slopping of water
up and down the iron. He juggles it
with all the collars, cuffs, pockets and sleeves,
shrugs blouses on to hangers, places them
in wardrobes, his hands precise and routine,
pretending he isn't leaving at last.
Her clothes will wait their turn till none remain,
just those hangers drooping like empty yokes.

# COMO UNA MIEL OSCURA

*"…como una miel oscura,*

*te siento…"*

– Antonio Gamoneda


I grew in your lips.
Their sudden absence
lies over my mouth,
shadowing my words
like a dark honey.

# ARTES CULINARIAS

(i) *Real chips*
Creamy dripping's polished
by constant, lilac gas
and spuds are chunked skew-wiff.

They reach a flour-stuffed crunch,
ready to tell my tongue
how childhood once tasted.

(ii) *Roast chicken*
I snuggle into mechanics,
chopping up breasts and rubbing flesh
from the neck, then scooping the heart.
A Sunday task, it absorbs me
till I find the flimsy wishbone.

(iii) *Lamb stew*
You peeled, you scraped, you sliced
all morning long, then set
the lot to simmer.

So what if he mentions
yet another girlfriend
just in case you make

a pass over coffee?
Catch the shine on his cheeks.
It vaults to his eyes

till he ducks and reaches
for another plateful.
Both your tongues round pearls

of succulent barley,
you've got him sharing more
than ever before.

(iv) *Choco relleno*
While skinning and sluicing,
I'm reminded how much
I've come to envy
cuttlefish.

It's so easy for them
to carry ink around
and keep it safe, close
to their heart.

(v) *Chocolate con churros*
The vat of oil must haze the air,
the batter sticky but slick.
He pipes it gently through the nozzle.
Spatulas dance as it ripples
in ring after fizzing gold ring.

Just after dawn his café steams.
Hunters, half-cut teenagers
and widows all hunch over cups
in the hubbub of the *churros*
being dunked in *chocolate*.

(vi) *Guisantes al vino tinto*
Crushed and sautéed garlic, smoked paprika,
a long dollop of wine and just-shucked peas –
this is still her dish and far more daring
than sly rummages for battered photos.
Especially now I'm serving it to you.

# FROM FARNHAM TO VILLALEJO

(i)
Turning circles in cul-de-sacs
are traps unless you know the town.
How many summers did I take
to map the paths that skulk
behind a fence or privet hedge?

I'm driving back past my old school,
past kids who droop their own way home.
Branches still beckon, the shadows
reminders of my teenage plan
to be done with this place for good.


(ii)
This is the only place I could live now.
It's lent me routines and even the hint
of a shared past. Aprils come with garlic,
Junes with peas. Shutters screech at dawn and dusk,
the clock tower dividing our days.

I wake and work and sleep to the perfume
of scorched pollen, crushed olives and mopeds.
As my mother-in-law summarises
another neighbour's life, both of us grin.
For a moment I almost belong.

# MATTHEW

Never shortened in Spain – if anything,
it's lengthened. My senses go taut
when you suddenly shift the stress

to its second syllable, reaching out
beyond my name. Your pitch alone
is enough to quicken my step.

# FROM THE DICTIONARY

(i)
*El girasol (nm)*

You swivel with the sun,
turning your back on me
as the afternoon slides
into evening.

(ii)
*La trashumancia (nf)*

On two Sundays a year, Madrid
seethes with countless migrating sheep
walking the streets unthinkingly
like Monday's flock of commuters.

(iii)
*Esperar (v)*

It begins as *Expect*
before becoming *Wait*
and ending up as *Hope*.

Language stamps on
language
till nothing else
is left.

# EXTRANJERO

Two decades on, perfection's lost
its distant lustre. My accent

seeps away. Every few minutes
I let some vowels tug me back home,

back towards the cadence of who
I am or was or was or am.

# HOME COMFORTS

Until you've lived in a country
full of kitchens full of saucepans
that slowly creak to the boil,
a kettle won't seem to whistle
like the owner of a loose dog
calling it back, calling it home.

# TWENTY YEARS APART

With a synchronised swivelling of necks
and a coughed silence, they welcome me in,
wincing as I order. Once I've sat down,
a soft hubbub resumes.

Ignore the smells, swap Spanish for English,
back streets of Villalejo for Oxford.
Muttered stories mirror muttered stories.
I'm still in the background.

## LA VISITA

The same portraits are standing guard
and the same piano keys grin
with yellowed teeth. Two rosaries
lie coiled on a sunlit table
like dozing, sated rattlesnakes.
*Everything's still where they kept it.*
Locking up and heading for home,
I whistle fiercely, wrestle off
the ransacking silence.

# THE KNIVES OF VILLALEJO

Blunted by the cloying dough of fresh bread
or transparent fat on a wafered ham,
they're speckled with rust, the handles darkened,
creaking while fingers force them down.

House after house, they wait for his whistle
as he pushes his bike from door to door.
He knows them well and whets them in seconds,
pinging the blade with a flourish.

And so they carry on chopping up days,
carving weeks, slicing months and dicing years
until they judder halfway through a stroke
and snap like over-sharpened lives.

# EL CASTILLO DE VILLALEJO

A spiralled street that's soon a track,
acrid air quivering, sunlight
ricocheting off panes and roofs.
I reach the jagged keep at last

where hillsides lean on hillsides
and lilac clouds hint at cool dusk.
Dark vines rise up against the sky
like the flailing arms of a man.

# DOS VINOS

(i)
*Tempranillo*

Bush vines protect me from the sun,
their leaves like hands, blocking harsh light.
From juice to wine, I macerate
until the skins stain me crimson,
ready me for a bottle.

Just watch me after every sip.
My glycerine falls down the glass,
leaving arch after arch behind,
a silhouetted cathedral
where you're worshipping again.


(ii)
*Gran Reserva*

I dozed in his cellar. He pulled me out
at a dinner once, and waited for her
while his taut fingers smudged my dusty neck.
He couldn't bear to keep me after that.

You saved me from the local merchant's shelf.
A whole decanterful of crispy air,
and I was born for this: a pair of mouths
to roll me across their tongues and share me.

# IN THE WINE TRADE

*'Buy on apples, sell on cheese.'*

(i)
*Back label*

*With raspberries and recently cut flowers*
*on an elegant and delicate nose,*
*our flagship Rosado then opens up*
*to a lip-smacking, refreshing palate.*
*It's ideal for lazy summer evenings.*

Forget those flash ideas
about discovering
a clean pattern of words
to renew and refresh
aromas and flavours.

Let yourself gently slide
into cutesy jargon,
coded blocks of language,
shortcuts that remind us
how we're supposed to feel.


(ii)
*At Prowein*

In a plush, anonymous room
just before the trade fair opens,
I reach for a tie, ignoring
the looming, wall-to-wall mirror.

I close my eyes and stall my thoughts,
and Dad's behind me once again.
We coax a perfect, funnelled knot
and pour me out as if to school.


(iii)
*Private brand*

From the liquid, the cork and the label
to the firm but far from crushing handshake,
the warm but slightly guarded tone of voice
the direct but never challenging glance
and tiptoed haggle round an extra cent,
everything's made to measure.


(iv)
*Final blend*

I pour and sniff, line up bottles
and row after row of glasses –
50/50, 60/40,
80/20, 90/10,
playing percentages for keeps.

When they're blended, neither can leave:
one lends smoothness; one offers bite.
They quell each other's weaknesses,
their bodies meshing and lifting.
I know this couple's right.

## MAKING PAELLA WITH DAVID

I watch his fingers learning how
to shell langoustines, exploring
their cartoon-alien faces
and train-track bellies. He giggles
at calamari tentacles,
snaps the glassy spines in half.

Just now he slung an apron on
and told me he'd help. Bell peppers
are staining the blade of his knife.
It's time to let ingredients
become a dish. He taps my arm.
Together we spark the gas.

# LEARNING THE LANGUAGE

David grabs the menu and points
at the words he recognises
like a delighted foreigner
on a first trip to the country
where he'll end up spending his life.

# AL ANOCHECER

David's still on the roundabout,
swaying joyfully up and down,
peeling paint with his fingernails.
This is a scruffy square – cheap bricks,
concrete benches and rusty bins –
but it's always been his playground.

My eyes switching on, off and on,
I smile and wave as he circles.
*Just one more go, Daddy, just one!*
I sweep him up. His cheek strokes mine
with my every step till we reach
our bolted, shadow-ridden door.

## AT CHIPIONA

Waves are singing across the sand.
A metre in, we're holding on,
our skin goose-bumped and thrilled by fear.

*Here comes a biggie!* you warn me.
My grip loosens and your voice sways
for the first time, ready to plunge.

# ¡CALLÉMONOS!

Decades ago I gave up saying why
I never say why I never say why.

Lamps in eyes are now my morse-code flashes
and interweaving fingertips my signs.

Listen as I stroke my message out.

# SPEECH RECOGNITION

*…busco… reconocerme desde mundos diferentes, desde cosas que sólo los poemas no habían olvidado.*

…I seek to…recognise myself through different worlds, through things that only poems hadn't forgotten.

– Julio Cortázar

(i)
*Gallery attendant*

Hour after hour spent around these pictures:
the clock, my watch, the shift-shift of my shoes
as I wait for coffee, then lunch, then tea,
the smoothing down of my skirt when schoolboys
study me more than any El Greco.

But worse are the hours spent in bed at night:
the churning shadows cast across my walls,
the moon behind like an albino's face,
its gloss of sweat or sainthood through the dark.
Trees become a crucifix in its hand.

(ii)
*Nothing as everything*

I was worried about the stain
a floppy, past-its-date sandwich
had smeared right across my lapel.

That was till I tried the key
and then fell in after it,
so I'm hunting round my rooms

on some scrawny git's tracks:
the whiff of bland lager
and sweet halitosis.

My drawers stand yawning,
mattress upside down.
Nobody had guessed

I'm worth less than
a spiv before
rationing hit,

and now there's
a kid who
thinks Goebbels

plays for
the Saints,
but who

knows
my
lie.

(iii)
*Last chance*

I'm stuck on a wonky trestle table
between a video tape of the Smurfs
and the 1989 *Good Food Guide*.
This is what things have come to after years
of being ignored as a last-ditch sop
from a jilted banker to his mistress.

I only want a single pair of hands
to stretch my spine and open me at last.
From what the volunteers are letting on,
either I'm found by a lonely reader
or pulped for envelopes. Just pick me up
and let my words wrap their legs round your heart.

(iv)
*Desaparecido*

Pillars and palm trees, the bonnet
of a Jag filtering through fronds
and no one looking down the lens
except me:

Mother's tying up her knuckles.
Father's standing in front, chest jutting
and a stubby index finger
shooting back.

No way am I folding my face
in sudden, vicarious shame.
I'd always wondered. Silence falls
like a dusk.

Click-click-clicks from the camera
echo the fugitive pieces
of a puzzle being slotted
into place.

During Videla's dictatorship, the Argentine army is alleged to have separated
prisoners (who often then become 'the disappeared' or '*los desaparecidos*') from their
offspring, before handing the babies over to officers for adoption.

(v)
*The ex*

There's no time for
dress rehearsals.

Miscast again,
I'm straight on stage,

and gulp. How long
should phone calls be?

How couched? Just what
is *cordial*

when it's at home?
Where is home?

(vi)
*Stepdaughter*

Months since he'd watched her cook and loop
a rogue strand of hair from her cheek,
months that had just concertinaed
like abandoned cars being scrapped.
This is how I still replay him,

clutching the door, back for that night.
She chopped a carrot, glanced and grinned.
I stroked my doll and let them talk,
not showing I'd noticed her arm
cup his head en route to the salt.

(vii)
*The patient*

*After Julio Cortázar*

Having squeezed your shoulders and tapped your cavities,
the doctor calms you down while you dress. You're nodding
in hasty hope. *Relax, a break is all you need.*

He stretches his legs, dapper trousers riding up
to reveal a glimpse of his shimmering stockings.
All of a sudden, those fears set in again.

(viii)
*Dad on the M25 after midnight*

Even before the front door's shut
he's in first gear – up past Tesco,
third exit from the roundabout
and onto the slip road at last.

This is where the housework and kids
recede, junction after junction.
He could head west, then north, then east
– with just a millimetric nudge

of the wheel – but he holds a lane,
perfecting this nightly circle.
It closes back in on his name.

# EPILOGUE

*For Josefa*


When you trace your wrinkles, criss-crossed
like the fine scars of unknown wounds,
and speculate how they got there;

when you're sure you hid the stained scarf,
the note and the bent bronze bracelet
for some significant reason;

you'll never quite remember what
you forgot, but you'll remember
you forgot.

## ACKNOWLEDGEMENTS

Magazines:
*Ambit, Coffee House Poetry, Current Accounts, The Frogmore Papers, Links, London Magazine, The Next Review, New Walk, Obsessed with Pipework, Orbis, Other Poetry, Poetry Nottingham International, Poetry Scotland, Rain Dog, The Rialto, Under the Radar* and *Seam.*

E-zines:
*And Other Poems, Clear Poetry, Good Dadhood, Ink Sweat & Tears, Mary Evans Picture Library Poems and Pictures, The Poetry Shed, Atrium Poetry* and *The Stare's Nest.*

Anthologies:
*The Best New British and Irish Poetry 2016* (Eyewear Publishing), *Hearing Voices* (Crystal Clear Creators), *The Needlewriters Anthology* (The Frogmore Press, 2015), *Blame Montezuma* (HappenStance Press, 2016)

An earlier version of 'From Farnham to Villalejo' won first prize in the National Library of Scotland's 'From Home to Beyond' poetry competition in 2014 and consequently formed part of the library's "Voices from the Commonwealth" display.

'Instructions for Coming Home' was a prizewinner in the 2009 Plough Prize.

Thanks are due to Helena Nelson of HappenStance Press for permission to reprint a number of poems from two pamphlets, *Inventing Truth* (2011) and *Tasting Notes* (2012).

Thanks to Richie McCaffery, John Field and Alexandra Payne for help and support.

**CO** **EYEWEAR** PUBLISHING

EYEWEAR'S TITLES INCLUDE

EYEWEAR
POETRY

**ELSPETH SMITH** DANGEROUS CAKES
**CALEB KLACES** BOTTLED AIR
**GEORGE ELLIOTT CLARKE** ILLICIT SONNETS
**HANS VAN DE WAARSENBURG** THE PAST IS NEVER DEAD
**BARBARA MARSH** TO THE BONEYARD
**DON SHARE** UNION
**SHEILA HILLIER** HOTEL MOONMILK
**MARION MCCREADY** TREE LANGUAGE
**SJ FOWLER** THE ROTTWEILER'S GUIDE TO THE DOG OWNER
**AGNIESZKA STUDZINSKA** WHAT THINGS ARE
**JEMMA BORG** THE ILLUMINATED WORLD
**KEIRAN GODDARD** FOR THE CHORUS
**COLETTE SENSIER** SKINLESS
**ANDREW SHIELDS** THOMAS HARDY LISTENS TO LOUIS ARMSTRONG
**JAN OWEN** THE OFFHAND ANGEL
**A.K. BLAKEMORE** HUMBERT SUMMER
**SEAN SINGER** HONEY & SMOKE
**HESTER KNIBBE** HUNGERPOTS
**MEL PRYOR** SMALL NUCLEAR FAMILY
**ELSPETH SMITH** KEEPING BUSY
**TONY CHAN** FOUR POINTS FOURTEEN LINES
**MARIA APICHELLA** PSALMODY
**TERESE SVOBODA** PROFESSOR HARRIMAN'S STEAM AIR-SHIP
**ALICE ANDERSON** THE WATERMARK
**BEN PARKER** THE AMAZING LOST MAN
**MANDY KAHN** MATH, HEAVEN, TIME
**ISABEL ROGERS** DON'T ASK
**REBECCA GAYLE HOWELL** AMERICAN PURGATORY
**MARION MCCREADY** MADAME ECOSSE
**MARIELA GRIFFOR** DECLASSIFIED
**MARK YAKICH** THE DANGEROUS BOOK OF POETRY FOR PLANES
**HASSAN MELEHY** A MODEST APOCALYPSE
**KATE NOAKES** PARIS, STAGE LEFT
**JASON LEE** BURNING BOX
**U.S. DHUGA** THE SIGHT OF A GOOSE GOING BAREFOOT
**DICK WITTS** THE PASSAGE: POST-PUNK POETS
**MATTHEW STEWART** THE KNIVES OF VILLALEJO
**SHELLEY ROCHE-JACQUES** RISK THE PIER
**PAUL MULDOON** SADIE AND THE SADISTS